Life Between the Stitches

Best Wishes to Marlow and Lorraine

Life Between the Stitches

By

Evelyn Ruth Knoff

Evelyn Ruth Knoff

Enjoy!

Copyright © 2008 by Evelyn Ruth Knoff

ISBN 0-7414-4419-4

Published by:

PUBLISHING.COM

1094 New DeHaven Street, Suite 100
West Conshohocken, PA 19428-2713
Info@buybooksontheweb.com
www.buybooksontheweb.com
Toll-free (877) BUY BOOK
Local Phone (610) 941-9999
Fax (610) 941-9959

Printed in the United States of America
Printed on Recycled Paper
Published January 2008

Acknowledgements

Special thanks to:

My late husband who encouraged me to write "by all means"

Green Lake Christian Writer's Conference in Wisconsin

Very Special thanks to Melanie Rigney, Owner of "Editor for You"
 and former editor of Writer's Digest, for her initial copy editing for this book

Grateful thanks to my son David Knoff as Contributing Editor and for
 computer layout work

Photograph of Olivia's Doily for book cover by Michael Parezo/Gene's Photo Studio
Photograph of author written permission given by Olan Mills Portrait Studio

Patterns used for works seen on pages as follows:
 Angels, page 70 et al, variation based on pattern from Van Beria,
 Scandinavian Imports, 217 W. Water St, Decorah, IA 52101.

 Buttonholed Doily, page 12, from *Hardanger Embroidery Favorites I*, p. 47
 Small White Square, page 26, from *Canadian Prairie Hardanger*, ©1995, p. 15
 (both from Nordic Needle, see below)

Charts on page 16 taken from *Hardanger Embroidery Favorites I*, ©1977,
Rosalyn Watnemo, Sue Meier, Nordic Needle, 1314 Gateway Dr, Fargo, ND 58103.
800-433-4321 www.nordicneedle.com Permission granted by Rosalyn Watnemo
and Susan Meier

Contents

PREFACE

Walking or strolling from the Bauer Lodge at Green Lake, Wisconsin, I took time to stop and study some flowers. Most were absolutely beautiful---good color, good arrangement and they were placed carefully giving distinction to each other.

Then I noticed a yellow one—maybe a daisy, but now quite faded. Half or more of the petals were missing, worn out I guess.

But that flower raised its head proudly among the rest. It was reaching toward the sun and surviving quite boldly.

This I likened to myself—quite worn, with a little less color amidst the rest of the strong plants and flowers. The plant is still standing, as I am—reaching for the sky, anticipating the day and happy for the beautiful ones around me. I'm glad they don't pluck me or mow me down, so I am bravely and boldly maintaining the place that I have in God's great flower garden.

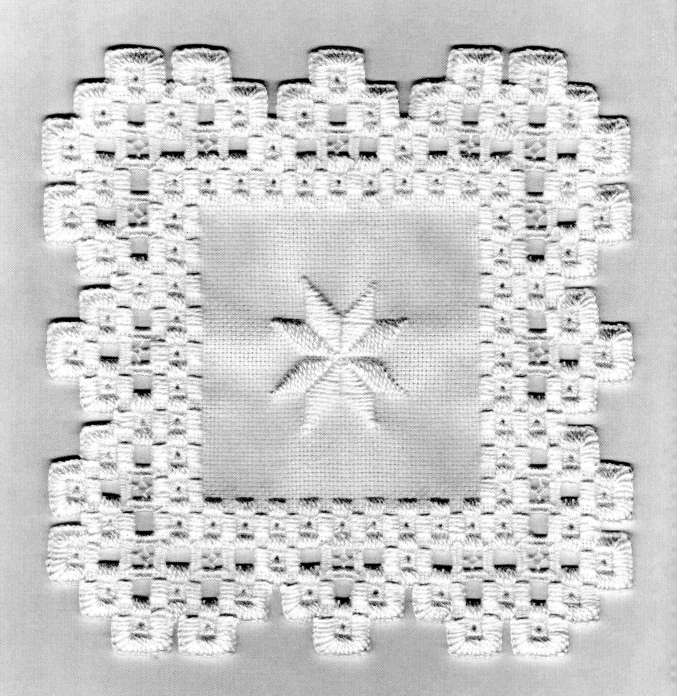

THREADS

Downsizing is underway.

Three things in life are certain:

Death, and Taxes, and Downsizing.

We live, we downsize, we die (and what we leave behind
      they downsize some more.)

If I were twenty-two, I wouldn't be writing this.

I'm eighty-seven years old now. And I'm downsizing again. That's why I'm writing this to you today. So I might not be totally discarded in the process, and what is of most value will remain.

This is taken from my journal 27 years ago (you may call it my "DOILY JOURNAL"):

DOILY JOURNAL
"It is dark down here. My brothers and sisters and I have gathered here in the cellar of my Mother's house to decide...what to do with the things left over from my Mother's lifetime of service."

Mother's cellar had traditionally contained excellent food—rows of canned vegetables, meats, pickles and jellies. Now it is different. Mother Olga is gone and her possessions are going into the hands of her children. After everything is decided, only the Hardanger doily remains. It looks so lost and forlorn.

The old doily stretches from its cellar floor to give me one last smile as I contemplate casting it aside. It does not look very enticing while crumpled and torn and lying on the dirt floor.

"What can I do with it?" I ask myself.

"Not much in its condition," I reason.

My impulse is to say: "I'll see what I can do with it."

Family members in Norway have expressed this to me: "Evelyn" they said, "our women kept the fires going at night by supplying the small stove with firewood while their husbands were in the forest cutting down trees. They watched the children as they slept, thus protecting and caring for them." My heart bursts with love and warmth as I remember how they told me of the courage and faithfulness of these ancestors.

And skillful endeavors of my mother and grandmother taught me by example the joy of achievement. Grandmother Olivia brought the first doily from Norway. I was to learn through the years of her life a heritage lived on through our family.

DOILY JOURNAL Facts:

Hardanger embroidery originated in the mountainous area of Norway. Hundreds of years ago Norwegian women stitched doilies in very elaborate designs. Some patterns were used in national Norwegian costumes. It was with delight I visited this area of Norway in the homeland of my ancestors.

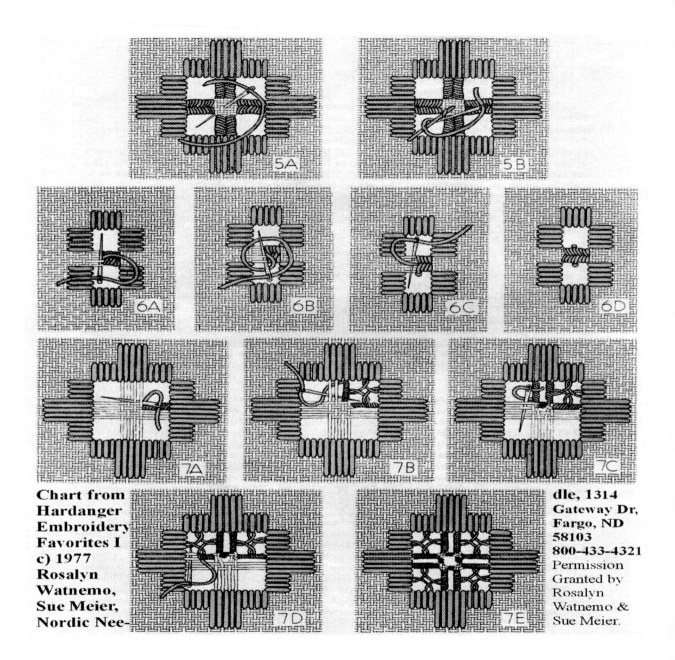

Chart from
Hardanger
Embroidery
Favorites I
c) 1977
Rosalyn
Watnemo,
Sue Meier,
Nordic Nee-

dle, 1314
Gateway Dr,
Fargo, ND
58103
800-433-4321
Permission
Granted by
Rosalyn
Watnemo &
Sue Meier.

When I look at Grandmother Olivia's doily,

I see
Life Between the Stitches

You may see
intricate patterns, wrappings, and cutouts.

I see life.

You may see a discarded doily.

I see my Grandmother Olivia.

BESTEMOR OLIVIA

The Norwegian word bestemor means the best mother or grandmother and she was mine.

I wish I could have trudged along behind Olivia as she rushed up the hill to the waiting horse and buggy. Olivia Luka Bredeson was leaving the Luka home for good at the age of seventeen. Bestemor Olivia Luka Bredesen was the oldest of eleven children, born in the beautiful Finn Skogen forest of eastern Norway. She was ready to sail to the new country in North America. With her she had a hand-carved box made by her father with the numbers 1857 beautifully carved on it. The small, engraved box contained dried beef, bread and fruit for the food she would consume as she crossed the Atlantic Ocean. A plain brown wooden trunk held the rest of her possessions. Over her shoulder was a hand-knit black shawl. In her eyes were tears but she would not look back. The new land of America was before her. Norway was experiencing a famine partly due to the fact that there was a severe famine in Ireland. Norwegian men could no longer go there for the potato harvest to earn extra money for their family's survival.

Olivia was one of many who sought help in a new land. The first member of the family to leave, it was a sacrificial moment for all. She walked to the wagon, loaded herself onto it to make the trip to the railroad station. From there she would journey to the seacoast and begin the two-month ship ride. She could only pray for what lay before her.

Her first placement in America was in Pittsburg, Pennsylvania where she worked for a laundry businessman. He had paid her fare on the ship in exchange for one year's work in his laundry. The first English words Grandma learned were "wash" and "iron." Young Americans laughed after they asked her to open a door in the laundry and an ironing board fell on her head. Bestemor tearfully told me this story many years later.

After one year, she moved to Wisconsin in the Viroqua area. Here were friends from Norway and here she met Anton Hanson Barstad who was to be her husband in a short time. Before they could be married, Anton went west to "sit on the land" for one year and claim the homestead near Bridgewater, Dakota Territory. Since he was too young to settle this claim alone, his mother Karen Tonette Barstad went with him for the first year. Together Anton and Karen built a homestead for the new couple to settle on. They built a dwelling before returning to Wisconsin. He married his bride and brought her to the farm three miles east of Bridge-water which at that time was named Nation City.

Olivia carried on Norwegian traditions. Over the years one could see her wonderful background shining through. She made sunbonnets from a Norwegian pattern. Her cake plate had an interesting story. She made a lovely white cake with lemon filling. (I ate cake made from this same recipe many years later in Norway. It was delicious with lemonade.) Grandma cut and stamped the lemon slices in a wooden bowl, added sugar and then called us, the grandchildren, to rush to the windmill and bring a pail of cold water from the well. It was definitely as cold as ice water is today. The drink was completed. We had walked a long mile from the parochial school and feasted on the drink and the cake.

The way that Bestemor got that cake plate was interesting. She told Grandpa "the other women in the Ladies Aid have cake plates on a stand and here I come with my flat plate." Soon, Bestefar brought a clear glass cake plate on a stand. She took one look at it and cried, "Anton, the other women have fancy ones with little glass balls all around the edge and this is so plain." Bestefar was a man of few words. He went to the barn, harnessed his horses, Barney and Bill, to the wagon loaded with oats. Soon he left for Bridgewater. He returned with a beautiful fancy cake stand that she used for many years. Yes, it had fancy glass balls around the edge. I wonder how many cakes were placed on that beautiful piece.

Mother Olga was the only remaining daughter of Olivia and Anton. Her sister, Inga, died at the age of twenty-three. Hence, Mother's family of eight became precious Barne Barn to Olivia. They are twice born or grandchildren. How we remember her coming the six miles to our home with her horse Barney pulling the buggy. As soon as she arrived, we children hurried to the stone foot warmer at the front of the buggy. We placed it near the heater to keep it warm until she left. Our older brothers took care of Barney giving him oats and a warm shed while Bestemor visited.

Next came the lemon drops in a big brown paper bag. There were enough to satisfy us all for a day or two. Then Olivia and her daughter visited in the Norwegian language. It was about the only time my mother got to use her native tongue. Grandma lovingly took us on her lap and shared with each one little stories.

On one occasion, Grandma gave her daughter thirteen dollars saying, "Buy a new linoleum rug for the front room." The kiddie car going around the center table had made a well-worn path in the old one. The next time she came, she said: "Where is the new rug?" This happened six times! Always, the money was urgently needed for something else. The seventh time she gave Olga thirteen dollars and said most emphatically, "Now buy the rug!" And Olga got a new green rug with big red flowers on it.

Olivia was a devout and dedicated Christian lady. She and Anton helped build Pleasant Prairie Church which was located three miles east of Bridgewater. I heard my grandma sing many solos and often leading parts in the choir. When she sang solos she walked to the center aisle of the church. She stood there dressed in her long black skirt and white long-sleeved blouse with the many pleats. Her hair was beautifully arranged at the top of her head. Her face looked angelic as she sang the solo "Behold the Host" in both English and Norwegian.

Into Bestemor's little Norwegian mission box went money she saved from the sale of cream and eggs. I heard Grandma tell that she saved the money from the Sunday eggs for missions. She also reported to mother that the hens laid more eggs on Sunday than on any other day. Almost monthly, it would be printed in the Morning Glory Magazine "Contributed for Missions by an anonymous donor from Bridgewater, South Dakota."

Among mother's castaways, I found an old doily—quite ragged and torn, but it was original Hardanger stitchery from Norway. It was more than one hundred years old. The 22-count linen was as good as new. How would I restore the broken stitches? So I went to my good friend Agnes Tenneboe to take lessons from her in Hardanger stitchery and she helped me restore the piece. Now framed on my living room wall, it is a treasure for all to see. It has led to a lively hobby for me because now I make doilies for my loved ones. By the way, Olivia also cleaned, carded and spun the wool to make warm mittens and clothing for all of us.

Olivia kept serving her Lord, her husband, daughter and grandchildren until December twenty-third, 1930, when she died following a stroke.

The word came to our home the day before Christmas. How awful it was that someone I loved so much and one who loved me even more would do this—to die just before Christmas! To me, a ten-year-old child, it was most confusing. How, oh how, could she do this to us? I wondered why she would die at Christmas time. All plans for our Christmas program were postponed. In our country church, where all the yule festivities were held, two large black blankets were thrown over the Christmas tree. The gifts and treats were also covered for Grandma's funeral. Our annual Christmas program, which was a highlight of the year, was postponed until January twenty-fourth, one month after Grandma left us. Then we received our gifts and treats. How could such a loving person do this to me? Maybe she thought more of the beautiful place she had gone to than of me.

It was many years before I fully understood that Bestemor did not lead the way but simply followed the Shepherd and joined the "Great White Host in Heaven Above" that she so often sang about. As I experienced the death of family members and friends in the years that followed, I learned that death is part of life much as the cutouts were part of a piece of hardanger. The example of others and their acceptance gave me confidence and I realized that she was called home. She did love me!

MINE MOR

Mother's strength could not be measured on earth. Only eternity will reveal her courage. She drew strength from her "sisu" or perseverance. She was the daughter of Norwegians Anton and Olivia Barstad Hanson. Her childhood influences were of her mother's Norwegian background.

Listening to stories of the beautiful trees and lakes of Norway awed my mother Olga. In the Dakota territory area it was difficult to grow trees and the virgin soil of homesteading only lent itself to cockleburs and mustard plants. The daughter of Norwegian-born parents, Olga heard about and experienced the hardships of pioneering. Her mother spoke of the pine trees and beautiful lakes in Kirkenaer area which I have visited three times. One is awed when you compare that wooded area of Finnskogen, the Finnish Forest, in Norway. Olivia and Anton found it hard to grow any variety of trees in the Dakota Territory where they homesteaded. They struggled to keep their possession clear of cockleburs and mustard plants.

Olivia and Anton had two daughters, my mother Olga and her younger sister Inga. The story goes like this:

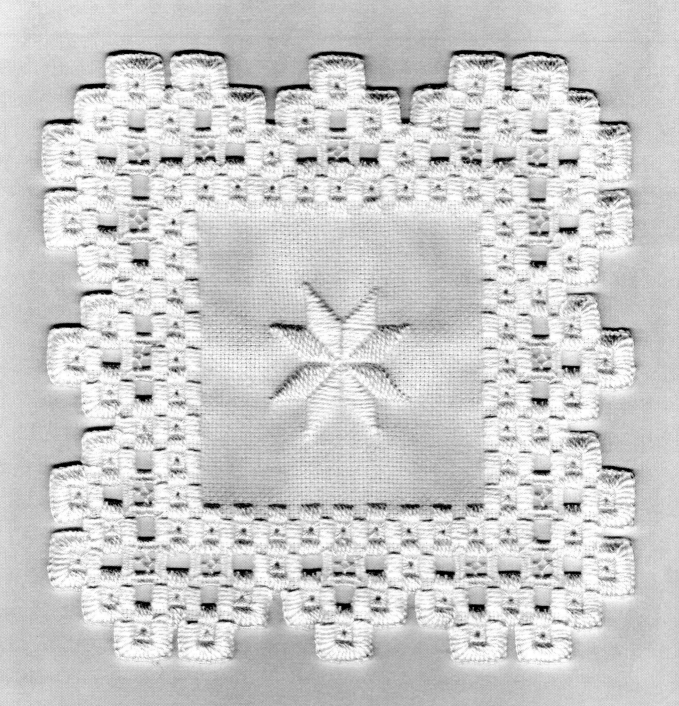

Olga came home from town one day. Inga was writing down her songs. She loved to write and memorize songs (and we still have one of her handwritten chorus books).

Twenty-something Olga was aflutter:

"Oh, Inga, I met someone today. His name is John. He is such a likeable person and a good businessman. He has the store in town."

"And I think he was very interesting."

Inga: "Was he handsome?"

"Well, he's very smart and inventive..."

and Olga thought a little while.

"But he's so homely!" and then they laughed.

This was the story Olga and John would tell for years after that, and then they would always laugh.

My mother Olga, a woman of beauty, married the man of her dreams. He was tall, lanky John of Russian and Dutch descent. John loved Olga dearly and boasted to all who came to our home of her beauty and her excellent cooking skills. She made the best butterscotch pies and fried chicken in the world. She treated her large family to large platters of corn on the cob. Countless offerings of vegetables came from her huge garden. The milk and butter, eggs, chicken and pork were all produced on a plot of land in a small town.

Born to Mother were nine children. The last one named Viola died when she was only nine days old. Eight children grew to adulthood. Mother grieved for her ninth child. Cousins and friends tried to comfort her, but she expressed strong love and stated that no one could replace her baby.

As mother nurtured her family, she used the principles of a doctor of psychology although she had only a sixth grade education. She was always positive. A desire to achieve and a good feeling of self worth was strengthened by her strong example. We were always the winners in our mother's eyes.

Widowed at fifty-eight after dad's difficult struggle with cancer, mother that same year saw three of her sons leave to serve in World War II. A daughter left to serve as a missionary nurse in Nigeria that same year. Mother purchased a better house and began to develop improved living conditions.

Entertaining on holidays was still big in mother's eyes. Her children came from far and near to be home for the holidays. At the end of a bountiful meal she would say: "Well, I hatched this goose from an egg, I raised it, I cleaned it and roasted it too. Haven't we had a good Thanksgiving?" At the age of eighty she bought a large new set of dinnerware. She liked to serve the meals on dishes that all matched.

As the years wore on, mother kept young. She pinched her cheeks daily to keep them rosy. She took pride in pretty hats and always wore good kid leather gloves and shoes.

She moved forty miles from her home town in later life to be nearer to her family. She adjusted well and went to her home in the summer as long as she could. She continued to make lovely quilts, aprons and bonnets. One of her daughters brought her a ball of yarn advising her to do something easier. After a short time, she threw the ball of yarn aside with the comment: "Maybe when I get old." She was only eighty-eight. Mother was ninety-three years old when she had surgery for a gall bladder problem. She consented only if I promised to be near her during the procedure. I stood outside the door of the surgical rooms of the hospital for the surgery.

In a nursing home following her illness, Mother still expressed a love for John. Her husband had preceded her in death by thirty-nine years. She wanted to be with him, with her baby Viola and with her Savior. She sang hymns and prayed to go home where she softly went to abide at the age of ninety-five.

DOILY JOURNAL Facts:

A blunt needle is used to make five stitches on a white linen 22-count piece of material. A kloster consists of five evenly woven stitches. Beginnings as well as endings in life must also be made very carefully. The influence and loving, tender care passed on from generation to generation produces a strong image on impressionable children, and it did on me.

Upon completion of a suitable background the design is begun. The foundation of life likewise is begun with patience and planning. Corner stitches must be turned exactly until all stitches are completed. Errors are corrected with great pain. Sometimes they have left an unforgivable impression. But if you don't take out the stitches all the way back to where the mistake was made... It'll still be there, and the mistake will seem to loom larger.

Papa

"Where are we going, Papa?" asked his four-year-old daughter.

"You'll see," he said as he gathered all the children from the house plus a few more into the car they called "Tin Lizzy."

It was a Model T and he started it by getting out and cranking the handle in the front of the car until the engine turned over and started. Sometimes it was a challenge to start and it could kick back. Sometimes people actually broke their thumb or wrist if it kicked back with the thumb on top rather than cupped under the handle, but it replaced the horse, and a horse could kick and kill a man, and many had. Anyway, the "Tin Lizzy" started up and they headed out through town and out past the grain elevator where Papa was the manager, out beyond the lowlands where the ducks and geese splashed in the sunshine among the bulrushes, past the sparkling waters of Silver Lake and into the country. Past the tall cottonwood trees on the lake on the left. What an adventure!

Finally, the car came to a large tent.
Oh my, what a tent! This was exciting.

Out next to the church in the country, the men had put up tent poles and raised a tent. And every night the men took the tent down and then raised it again for the next night.

The tent was tan-colored canvas and had fresh straw from bales for the floor. There was the murky smell of the gas lamps fastened to the poles. Each had a mantle and a wick to be lit. As evening came, a full harvest moon rose. And <u>if</u> it was really made of cheese, that night it certainly was the color of velveeta, and just as smooth.

Inside the tent, the women sat all dressed up and proper in their fine dresses and black high-top shoes, and they wore their hair up in a bun at the back of their heads. The men sitting with them wore hats which they took off indoors. The singing was enchanting to the little girl and there was a children's lesson. But after all the singing, the little girl's interest was overcome by her drowsiness, and she rolled under the wooden plank she had been sitting on and down to the straw floor, as a long talk lulled her slowly... slowly... slowly... into a sound sleep.

When she woke up it was dark.

"Papa, papa, where are you?" she cried.

It seemed like the whole world, or at least the whole tent had caved in around the little girl in the straw in the tent. What was a four-year-old to do? There wasn't anybody there.

But then she heard the familiar sound of the "Tin Lizzy."

First distant, then louder... louder... louder. It stopped. Then came the voice out of the dark:

"Evelyn, Evelyn, where are you?"

It was Papa. He had gone three miles down the road with his load of kids when he realized one was missing.

Could it be? Could she be somewhere around the tent the men had already let down?

Sure enough. There she was, crawling out from the straw under a flap of the tent--following the sound of her father's voice.

Papa's stern, concerned expression began to crack, and the edge of his lips crinkled upward until widespread sunshine broke out across his entire countenance.

Quickly he reached down with his big hands and picked her up to rest on his shoulder.

"Let's go home," was all he said.

And the velveeta moon smiled in approval... illuminating the way home in the car called "Tin Lizzy."

That was more than eighty years ago, and I was that little girl. I'll never forget that feeling of security in my father's love. Hearing his voice calling my name, and seeing his strong hands lift me up gave me a feeling of security that I have never forgotten.

And I know the time may soon come, as it has for all but one of my brothers and sisters so far, that I'll reach up and say, "Papa, papa, where are you?" Then I know that Jesus will reach down and place me on His shoulder and I will be safe from all harm. The sense of resting on my father's shoulder near to his heart gives me a great security in my Heavenly Father.

SECURITY

Supplying the needs of the family
Wheat ground to flour
Wheat that had been bartered
 For a corn husking job,
Taken to the colonies.
After ground,
 Stored at the top of the stairs
In large cloth bags.
Many great loaves of bread would follow.

Chopped wood piled high
By Dad and his boys
To supply the hard coal heater
To fight off the subzero weather.
 In the cellar, jars of veggies
Yellow cut corn would be doused
With homemade butter.
 Green beans to be fried French fashion
 Green peas we children picked,
Shucked and sampled.

Dill pickles, sweet pickles,
Beet pickles so red
Melons, pickles in brine
In a stone jar.

With a rock on the top.

A bin boarded up
Held potatoes for eight
Mashed, boiled, baked or fried

Plus lefse for the holidays to anticipate.

Out of doors, the dirt piled high
Around the house foundation
As cold days come
Water pumped and carried
Will cover the dirt

Freeze hard and fight off the cold.

Mom's goodies always ready
Butterscotch pies,
Cream puffs with filling
Superseded only by the
Cookies with raisin filling.

HOW GLORIOUS THE SECURITY FOR WINTER

RIDE WITH ME

I had a buggy ride with my Grandma early on. Barney, who was her calm and poised horse, pulled the buggy. She controlled him with her whip. Most of us listened to grandma including Barney. I enjoyed the slow and beautiful ride as we took the cream and eggs to a market in the nearby village.

At an early age, I rode with my dad as he took the family on short excursions around our small town. We were so proud to be the first owners of a car in Dolton. The car had "izing glass" windows. We peered through them while the rest of the town watched us go by. The speed may have been five miles per hour. Often at bedtime dad put the family in the car and drove around until we were sleepy. We arrived home, dressed in our nighties and were carried to our beds. What a safe and secure feeling!

Later, dad took us on trips to neighboring towns and states. One sunny day, I was left in the car while my parents visited relatives. We were parked at the top of a hill. I thought it would be fun to practice driving, so I sat behind the wheel and made big imaginary turns. Suddenly I was going down that hill headed for a small barn. Stepping on the clutch had started the car in movement, so reasoning, I quickly removed my foot.

Wow! The engine started. What an exciting crash as I reached the building at the foot of the hill. The damages were large but I received no punishment. My oldest brother repaired the building during the next week or two. I was a more experienced driver.

Childhood led to adulthood. After my dad's death, I drove the 1928 Chevrolet to surrounding towns. No driver's license was required.

In 1938 I rode in a one horse open sleigh in a prairie area in northern South Dakota. My first year of teaching in a rural school was delightful. On wintry days, the farmer loaded his two daughters and two neighboring girls along with me into the sleigh. He placed a horse blanket over us. As he stood at the front of the sleigh, I prayed constantly that he would not fall backward during the mile trip. I should have relished those rides more as they were very special.

MY LOVING FATHER

My father, John H. Dirks, was born of Dutch-Russian immigrants who came to the United States in 1847. Born in 1879, he never lived more than fifteen miles from his birthplace southeast of Dolton in Dakota Territory.

Stories of the time of his childhood in a sod house amazed me. Their homemade oven was out of doors. They twisted hay tightly to provide fuel for this oven. Their dad, Henry C. Dirks, made the trip of almost fifty miles in frigid weather across the prairies to Yankton to purchase necessities. Once the family was in need of salt and yeast for bread making. Henry wrapped his feet with paper, then with burlap many times before donning his skis for the cross country trip. In his pocket were two small coins. Arriving in Yankton, he was exhausted and hungry so he spent part of the money for a morsel of food. Hence, he headed back home   with only the yeast—no money for the salt. Nearer home, he stopped at a pioneer home, borrowed the salt until the next spring . They could again make bread with home-ground flour.

At a young age dad cycled ten miles to the fair in Bridgewater. There he saw Olga in all her beauty. She was standing behind a lemonade stand. John saw this most beautiful girl with her radiant smile, her rosy cheeks and flowing hair. She appealed to him, a tall lanky kid seven years older than her. He didn't even meet her that time, but one thing became evident to him as he left that place. He expressed it to his friend as they sped toward their farm home hear Marion. "If ever I marry," he said, "it will be to a girl like that." But it was a few years later that my Mother and Dad actually met. He was to tell this story at many dinner tables in the years that followed as a blushing Olga smiled and listened again.

Father told of the blizzard of 1888. He remembered that blizzard as he told his sons in the 1930's. As the family watched in awe, they dug a tunnel. This tunnel was dug from our kitchen window to the barn. When it was completed they could crawl through it to care for the animals in that barn. How I wanted to crawl through that tunnel!

Dad recalled tragedies of the '88 blizzard. Ropes were tied around family members as they left their home. They were connected to each other. Ropes were tied. Securely tied and holding on as well as they could, many came back to the house. Dad named neighbors whose lives were lost in that storm. A family near his home sent one after another to rescue brothers and sisters. They saw frozen bodies from the house to the barn the next morning.

Dad helped his parents in their old age and in their last illnesses. His brother Ben cared for them during the day and he watched over them at night. He learned tenderness and compassion at a young age. He was careful to help each of our family members in times of sickness including my mother who was often ill. Always he would come with a sack of fruit to soothe our fevers and pains. When I was recovering from pneumonia, he tried in three towns to find the fresh grapes I asked for. Finally, he returned with a can of white grapes and spooned them into my mouth. When an older brother was ill, he went to a farm near Freeman, had a small lamb butchered to make the broth he felt would be healing. This fresh broth saved my brother's life.

Dad liked business. In our home was a lovely shell thermometer from his business travels in Mexico. He sold many brands of products for a time. Then he went into business with his brother Cornelius in Bridgewater. Thus the Dirks-Gross Department store came into being. In that store the lovely clerk named Olga came under his employ. He made many changes in the store but he did not change Olga's position. She was to become a part of his life forever.

After their marriage, they settled in the small town of Dolton where dad became the proud manager of the Dolton elevator. Always interested in people, he knew the farmers from a large area. He served in that capacity until the depression of the 30s hit. Farm crops were diminished and many grain elevators were closed including his. Then he cared for the Dolton School and the Community church until his death.

With four sons and four daughters, plus a little nine-day-old Viola who was buried in Pleasant Prairie Cemetery, he worked hard to care for his family. While he was school custodian, he helped to shock and thresh grain for the farmers during summer vacations. Thus he increased his income and survived.

My father came from a Mennonite background. His immediate and extended family were founders of the Silver Lake Church. After their marriage, my parents drove to the Lutheran Church where mother was reared and her parents attended.

In our town was a Community church begun by the Sunday School Union. It was there, in his own words, that he became a "full-fledged Christian." At the age of fifty, he became a new creature. Many changes were made in his life. Filled cigar boxes were smashed and thrown into the hard coal heater. Never again did he smoke. Liquor bottles were smashed on rocks in the alley. Never did he drink alcoholic beverages again. Restitutions were made to farmers he felt he had wronged in the grain business. He drove in his old Chevrolet in the night to talk to farmers and pay them for wrongs done. A peace and joy came to him and he openly told of his love for Christ and the church. He worked and prayed for his family, his church and relatives until his death in 1942.

Our father watched the development and growth of his eight children with pride. When we brought home good report cards his joy was very noticeable. Beams of pride shone on his face when we won the spelling contests. He was thrilled as he was told of marriages, of careers and of business transactions that were taking place. Everyone worked hard at jobs that could be found. He boasted of the two grandchildren he was to know before his death.

After one year of teacher training in a junior college, I left home to teach in a rural school. This school was three hundred miles away. He had tried to help me get a position nearer home. Jobs were at a premium. I was fortunate to get this fifty five dollar a month job. I had reached the age of eighteen in May so I could sign my own contract. He was excited for me and did not let me know of his apprehension until years later. He took me early one morning to catch a ride to my new school. There was a very tender look in his face as he waved a friendly good-by to me.
  That was the winter he wrote letters to me. When I received my check each month I sent a small amount home and always included a small donation to the church. I received a friendly reply and a one page letter ending with a scripture verse "In quietness and confidence shall be your strength" and "Underneath are the everlasting arms." Always the letters were signed "Your Love-ing Father, J.H.Dirks."

It was traumatic when I received a letter in December of 1941 stating "Your Dad is seriously ill. He did not go to church on Sunday." Dad had not missed one service in his church for thirteen years. By Christmas time he was hospitalized in the Mitchell Methodist Hospital. I spent my Christmas vacation in the hospital with him. On March sixteenth , he left this world of suffering and sorrow for a heavenly home prepared for him. Friends and relatives crowded our home. An uncle said as he put his arm around me "Your dad left you more than a million dollars. He left you a good name." A farmer comforted me with these words: "If your dad isn't in heaven, there isn't any heaven." He had made a clear statement of his faith. Dear mother stayed close to his side until the last moment. She told me that when the nurse pronounced him dead she audibly heard the voice of the minister who had married them so many years earlier saying, "Till death do us part."   **Yes, he was my "Love-ing Father."**

BOARDING OUT

In 1938 I was reaching toward my first home away from home. I joined three classmates to search for school positions. My concerned and worried Dad had left me on an early morning at a farm home for my ride north. I was barely eighteen years of age and the farm area I would see would be strange to me. Our journey took us hundreds of miles toward the north. We were going to an area where coyotes awaited us. Farm folks were ready to receive four teachers.

Four young people were venturing forth in search of a life position. One year of Normal Teacher training and a strong desire was all we had. Being one of those four young "would be" teachers was very challenging. In the County Courthouse we sat in a cold hallway. A farm family carefully scrutinized us and made their choices.

I was the fourth one of the group to be chosen and I squirmed and edged back and forth on the wooden bench. There seemed to be no future for me when suddenly a family of four appeared. Two young girls smiled at me and soon the family chose me as their teacher. The business agreement was quickly transpired in the office with only a signature. We left the building to enter an old car. No way but that the new school marm would sit beside the farmer while his wife and two daughters sat in the back seat. He carefully dusted the seat and closed the car door. I was off to seek my fortune. I felt very insecure.

The miles covered were seemingly forever. Then we arrived at the small farm house. I was carrying the one suitcase that held my possessions. I was shown to a small bedroom that I would share with one of the girls who would be my seventh grade pupil.

A welcoming meal was prepared and one could wish for no better. A table grace was said and love was everywhere. The question in my heart was: "Will this teacher measure up to what will be expected of her?"

Daily after the long walk to the small square white schoolhouse, I eagerly entered to prepare for a full day of work. Within an hour, eleven anxious and excited children greeted me. In the late afternoon with all classes ended, all school chores were completed and up the hill to the farmhouse I wearily walked. The eleven children walked in several directions to their homes. One seventh grade boy proudly mounted his pony and rode in a north-westerly direction.

Exceptional times occurred when snowstorms and dust storms filled the air. When severe storms arrived, the farmer came with his sleigh pulled by a horse with a blanket over his back. Another horsehair blanket was placed over the heads of the teacher and his two daughters.

All view was hidden as we quietly sat there trusting that the farmer would not fall back on the passengers.

Included in the evenings after a delicious supper was homework and handwork. I pieced together my first quilt top that winter.

The night's rest ended with the man of the house stirring up the wood in the heating stove. With only a curtain in the doorway, the supplying the fuel and cranking up the heater was rather noisy. Awakening me also was the water landing on my face as the heat caused condensation from the cold plasterboard ceiling.

As I began the day, I remembered the night with the coyotes howling in the distance I also remembered my mother and father and the brothers and sisters I left behind. I had not much time for loneliness as I prepared for the duties of the day. Duty called me into action. All eighteen years of my life came into play as I worked day by day. Each morning I faced the day with a smile on my face. I was justly proud of the four-piece ukulele band I organized and trained. When they won in the county competition, I was joyous. After eight months, I was quite satisfied with a job well done. The children had advanced in their studies. I had earned the respect of the community and I was anxious to return to my parental home. I learned much from my students and from teacher's meetings.

When spring came, three of the original group of teachers were ready to return south to our homes. One had quit and taken the bus home after one week In the old suitcase I had brought with me in the fall were my possessions. I had added a large cardboard box containing the lunch pail and some warm clothing that I had purchased during the winter.

"No," said the housewife when she saw me.

"Leave that box here. It can be in the attic until you come back in the fall." I was a shocked young lady who thought quickly and made a sudden decision.

"Oh," I said, "I can't come back in the fall. I am going to college."

THE PROMISE BOX

On the Saturday following our wedding, December 31, 1942, we began our trip back to South Dakota. Now we would begin our life together in the church ministry Leonard had begun in July. The pleasant weather and good trip will always be remembered. When we stopped at gas stations, cafes and stores, people were informed that we were newlyweds. He grinned from ear to ear. It didn't seem to impress the people very much. I may have blushed at times.

Almost one hour out of Lincoln, Nebraska, he said, "Evelyn, there is a Promise Box in the pocket there. Why don't you choose a Promise?" I did. The promise was "If two of you agree about anything you ask for, it will be done for you by my Father in heaven." Matthew 18:19.

It was war-time, but we had enough gas-rationing coupons to get us safely home. Our first groceries were purchased at a town near home. We looked at each other wondering who had the money to pay for the loaf of bread, bottle of milk and a ring of bologna. Each of us emptied our pockets and it was turned out just right! Only a token of the great days that lay ahead of us!

At the parsonage, I was ceremoniously carried over the threshold. I was a little shocked as we entered the main room of the house. I had not seen it previously as that would not have been proper in those days. It seemed to be the kitchen. Adjoining it was a large living room. Due to the cold weather, the bed had been moved into the living room. He assured me it would be changed when warm weather came. Off the kitchen, was a "cob" room. I was a little surprised when I opened that door which was boarded up so cobs would not fall into the kitchen.

The house was soon warm and we were choosing food from the well-supplied pantry. Soon the Pastor was reviewing his sermon for the next morning. We had chosen a duet we would sing for the service.

I felt it was my God-given duty to prepare a bountiful breakfast the next morning. What it lacked in quality it made up for in quantity: oatmeal, toast, pancakes and a few other items adorned our table. I soon learned that he liked his toast just a little dark brown. I believed that for a few weeks until I realized I had a very kind and understanding husband.

Only a wooden walk separated the house from the church. Soon we were practicing our duet. Singing and supplying the stove with fuel occupied some time. We kept watching the front door but no one was entering the church. Rather to our chagrin, we now noticed a fierce storm was raging out of doors. Back to the house we went. Since we had no telephone, Leonard went to the village store to call a church member. "The weather is too severe for anyone to come to church", he said, "Lock the door and we'll see you next Sunday."

Some more eating and arranging and we began the journey to my hometown where I would continue my teaching career on Monday morning.

HOME FOR THE NEWLYWEDS

Tenderly carried over the threshold

His strong arms lifted his treasure

Proud and happy the couple

Entering the bachelor parsonage

The bride's eyes filled with surprise.

The manse had been nicely prepared

Welcoming the new couple

Hubby had scrubbed the kitchen

Cans of food lined up in rows

A kitchen to behold!

An arched opening to the living room

Showed a bed in the parlor

Frigid weather necessitated this

It would all change when warm weather came.

Another shock as I opened a door

Revealing a large room full of corncobs

To supply the Monarch kitchen stove

Bounded up by boards so none could

Fall into the kitchen.

With all the good wishes

And all the faith our spirits rose

From seeing the home where the pastor dwelt

This house could be seen

Only after we were wed.

Appropriateness counted in those days.

Morning dawned

With snow and cold.

For the wedding had been

On the last day of the year.

A bountiful breakfast began the day

This lady showed all her cooking skill.

He was treated to fruit, oatmeal

Toast, pancakes and coffee.

His love caused him to quickly

Assure me that the toast was great

He liked very dark toast.

Much purchased at the last store

Before reaching home.

All the essentials were on hand.

A couple in the clouds

We both emptied our purses.

To begin life together.

Much wonderful food would follow

In the years to come.

Assured we had been led to each other

The verse he had chosen

As he left his training in Chicago

"I being in the way, the Lord led me."

Only a boardwalk separated the

House and the church.

Ahead of the congregation

We made our way

Once inside on this cold day

We went to the piano to rehearse

The duet we would render this Sunday morn.

Singing, laughing, longingly we hoped

The doors would soon open

Beginning time came and went.

A call is made from the country store.

Members absent give a negative reply

"The snowstorm is blowing wildly

Close the doors. See you next Sunday."

Chagrined but not defeated

Back to the parsonage we went

Facing a wedded life of 56 years

Memories alive of our first home and church.

The Brothers

In northeast North Dakota, where my husband grew up, they said it was so flat you could see eternity from there.

It was a cold wind that blew across that flat, desolate prairie as little Leonard's mom, Martha, wrapped the scarf around his neck, gave him a hug, and sent him off with a hearty "Vaer sa god, lite barn" (vay-er so go, lee-ta barn) Norwegian for something like "Here you go, little one" and he trundled off the mile to school in the winter snow.

And in the years following, the scarves were passed down like so many things are in a family with six brothers.

Some years later it was instant recognition when, with playful mischief in his eyes, the third brother, Leroy, came up behind his brother Ervin (who was sitting near his M4 Sherman tank on a battlefield in the middle of Europe) and playfully threw the scarf over his brother's shoulder.

What a surprise: to be on the battleground on Christmas Eve and your brother finds you there!

"Here's your scarf, brother. You may need it."

"No, you keep it, you need it yourself."

Being the older brother, Ervin insisted Leroy have the scarf. And Leroy had brought it for his brother. So they decided. Taking out a knife, they cut the long scarf in two, and said when they met again they would sew it together.

It was the most cold and snow in memory that winter in Europe. And since the advance had been so rapid since D-day, the expectation was that the war would be over before Christmas, and so the warm clothes for winter and even the packages from home were not brought in.

Tank warfare in the battle for Europe was tough. And the cold and mud first, and then the deluge of snow followed.

Sometimes behind the lines you never knew how much waiting you do in war, and then it all happens at once.

Ervin had a buddy in his squad named Cal—they had become fast friends. When Ervin got orders to be called up to the front, his buddy Cal thought about it a little bit, and then he volunteered:

"I'll go. I'll go in place of Knoff. He has a wife and kids. I've got no one waiting for me. No one will miss me. Let me go."

And so he did.

But first, Erv said to Cal, "Here, take my scarf, you may need it" and he saw him off.

It was just a few days later word from the squad came back with the news. "When he got to the front, Cal sent this scarf back for you. He thought you may need it. He was killed in the battle a couple days ago."

And the scarf was passed on again as it often is with brothers.

Only one mistake Cal made. In the "band of brothers" as the soldiers were sometimes called, they weren't all brothers by blood—except they were by their own blood.

And Cal was wrong. He did have family at home, waiting for him. Only he never got to meet us. It seems we were his family too, we just didn't know it yet.

It was two years later Leonard and I went to Glenwood for the homecoming reunion. And Ervin and Leroy brought their two halves of the scarf and sewed them together.

I'm sure it may not have been the most difficult sewing ever done, although <u>so</u> meaningful.

But the sacrifices made, like those that brought those two pieces of scarf back together again, should make us all be forever grateful.

DOILY JOURNAL

One does not always choose. One accepts and loves the experiences that come. Sometimes they are planned and more often they come as wonderful surprises from the Father in Heaven. My life had been planned by the Lord. I was in the way and the Lord led me. As things develop in the stitchery, a finish is in view. Buttonholing the entire edge is used to seal and complete the doily. Without the closure that the edging provides even the most elaborate piece would unravel and be worthless. Our lives likewise mature and grow as God's plan becomes realized. Slowly but surely we grow in our spiritual life as we serve the Master daily.

Cutting the lines and drawing the threads can be very painful. I wash my hands and take a deep breath before beginning this process. It is risky but very necessary to form a good foundation for the design. I wonder as I realize the process in my developing life and the steps it has taken to give me my personal design.

The beauty of adolescence is known only to those who have carefully reached the stage of weaving and wrapping the cotton threads into a solid and becoming piece.

A TIME OF STORM

I like that song about a "Shelter In the Time of Storm." It tells of security. It makes me feel so safe. It helps me face the reality of the storms that will some day appear on my horizon. Never did I think there would be a literal storm to challenge my buoyant and enthusiastic self.

It all happened on March seventh in 1950 on the South Dakota prairies. My husband pastored a village church in the southeastern part of the state. He was from North Dakota where snow filled the sky and covered the ground much of the winter. The church was less than fifty miles from my birthplace. We both felt well equipped to meet any challenge that winter could offer us.

A member of the Board of Education came to the parsonage on an early March day with a plea for help. "Could you teach our school for three months?" he asked. What a good opportunity to work for only three months. It would be helpful to the community who were in desperate need of a teacher. Before my marriage, I remember good experiences I had teaching in rural and small town schools. We decided that my husband would take me six miles to the school and return for me each afternoon at 4:30. Our two sons, aged five and one, would be with him.

On March 7th we arose early. It was the second day of the new project. Our oldest son stated that this was the day he would visit school. He was almost six years old and ready to begin his own classes at Sunshine School near our home. I packed an extra sandwich, banana and cookie. This plan changed quickly. When we started the trip, he decided to stay with his dad and brother. So I entered the schoolhouse alone.

Soon all the good things were happening. Eleven anxious scholars began the process of learning. I saw brothers and sisters helping younger children throughout the day. All seemed interested in making progress. Smiles were exchanged between teacher and pupils. The first recess came. Then more learning until lunch time. Lunch pails were quickly produced from the wooden shelves in the hallway. Smells of bananas and oranges were in the air. Some help was needed for little fingers to peel the oranges. I sat with my double lunch in front of me of me and ate about half of it.

The children had their after-lunch exercise out-of-doors. I heard much laughing as with difficulty the door opened at one o'clock. A high wind had risen.

Soon teacher and students were again completely absorbed in learning. It took structure to keep the day's activities moving rapidly enough to have all classes for each grade level completed by four o'clock. A short afternoon recess proved to be only more difficult due to the wind.

Now it was four o'clock. The clock on the wall above the stone water cooler told us all we must be ready for parents who were arriving to pick up their children.

Then it came. Suddenly the sky was filled with the white stuff as though tons of flour had been dumped on us. Parents quickly rushed their children into cars to get them safely home before the spring storm worsened. Several people kindly asked me how I would get home. With full confidence, I responded that they were picking up their children and my husband would be able to come for me in thirty minutes.

As the school emptied, the winds increased, the sky became darker and snow filled the air. The small pot-bellied stove in the middle of the room still had heat in it. The chalk boards were erased, books were returned to their places and the embers in the stove began to die down. With fuel out-of-doors, I looked about uneasily. Peering out of the western window, I asked myself when he would come. I watched for the car lights. I did not realize that the storm was raging even more fiercely around our home where a husband and two small boys prayed for my safety.

Oh yes! Communication-we had it! The country phone line began to be active. A concerned mother called to inform me that her husband would come to my rescue. Only too soon she called back to say that the car would not start. On the country line were two more mothers. One asked if I could ride a tractor. I felt that I could do that. Soon the dear lady called to inform me that the tractor was laden with heavy snow.

There was always a way. Then a family offered their high school son and his father to come for the rescue. He had just been picked up at school and the car was still running. I knew all things were working together for good. The front lights of that car were beautiful. My faith was rewarded as the two of them drove into the schoolyard, and I quickly rushed to the still-running car. As if it seemed to sense my presence, immediately as I arrived the motor stopped abruptly. "Are you good to walk?" were the only words I heard. So, thinly clad and with only silk hose on my legs and no boots, we started the journey. Not knowing where we were going, I stayed in line with the two rescuers who were risking their lives to save mine. We kept walking except for times when the wind completely controlled our movements. With a one hundred mile an hour wind, we struggled to stay on the ground. Sometimes we were thrown off course, but we proceeded down the rural road in a southerly direction.

At one point, the wise farmer asked his son if we could still see the telephone line wires. The negative answer was causing some despair in all of us. A strong feeling came over the farmer that if we had lost our way there was no use to continue the two-mile journey. I heard the son simply say "get going" as he slapped my cheek, put my purse on his arm and prodded us on our way. Snow was blinding us, wind pushed us and there seemed to be no hope. The snow was freezing on our faces and legs. We were overcome by the elements of the air.

Then it happened! I felt a sudden quietness as we trudged along the side of a grove of trees. The Ira B. Sankey song, written one hundred years earlier, came from my childhood memories:

"Jesus is a Rock in a weary land,
A shelter in the time of storm."

Then the Courage! Then the Hope! I felt them carry me the last part of the way. Then the journey ended with the opening of the farmhouse kitchen door to a completely ice-covered trio. The lady wondered if there could be a person in that block of ice and snow that was pushed onto her kitchen floor. I sensed numbness as the otherwise red coat was pulled off me. I felt relief at the sensation of skin going along with my stockings as they were removed. What a blessing for all of us that they could contact a doctor in the nearby town just before the country phone line broke down. Cold applications to my legs produced steam. Watching the steam arise from myself, I lay on the kitchen floor of friends I had just met.

All night I lay in an upstairs bedroom listening to the wind howl and rage. I felt an unusual peace as these words were ringing in my ears:

> "The raging storm may round me beat
> A shelter in the time of storm
> We'll never leave our safe retreat
> A shelter in the time of storm."

At last dawn came. I found my place at the window seat watching a bright sun arise. The driveway was blocked with snow banks. My eyes peered past the driveway as I saw my husband slowly and cautiously make his way walking through the drifts. He looked haggard. I wondered where my boys were. He had found an empty schoolhouse early that morning and he searched nearby farms for me.

When we met at the kitchen door, the big smile on his face was all the assurance I needed.. Our two sons were being cared for by kind neighbors and we were all safe from the storm's harm. God's very special angels had protected each of us. All were sheltered.

"Be Thou our Helper ever near"

HOME ON THE PRAIRIE

The smelly cattle truck pulled up to the front
door of the parsonage.

Into it went my light blue sofa and chair,

Earned with my hard earned money

Also the spinet piano found itself there

Along with items-unaccountable

Items so rare.

Adventure being my middle name,

I watched it all with glee.

Books, clothes and dishes,

with toys in the car,

My small family too found their spot.

A light trailer following the car carried

the surplus.

Several long hours of travel brought

Us to that prairie location,

Outside the car to view the scene:

Prairie grass, no trees,

no flowers or bushes.

Kind hearts and hands painted the house.

Indoors and outdoors.

Remaining hours of the day

saw us unpacking,

All possessions jammed into the place_

One bedroom, one small study became

Sleeping places for us three.

Tomorrow will give us new strength:

New grace, enthusiasm and vigor.

Sleep came finally in spite of what we face.

Until midnight when a small voice

Called from the crib in the study:

"When are we going home?"

Morning and many mornings came

All things began to work together for good.

Trees were planted but did not grow,

A small garden struggled for life.

Grass abounded and it was green..

Only prairie grass grew there.

Two years and a cistern was dug.

Water would be hauled from a small town.

No more hauling water from nearby farms

No more going to neighbors to wash clothes.

Music and the Word

Thrived in the small Church.

Brother and Sister they called us.

The first wedding and the bride's ring

Would not go on the swollen finger,

The first funeral at which graveside

I wept with all my heart.

Until a dear old lady said,

"Weep not so much now.

Wait for your own family."

I watched quietly as friends,

With shovels in their hands,

Closed the grave.

The best that could be offered

Brought to this needy couple

Twenty spring chickens given in love

By a widow woman with full faith in God.

"We cannot take so many of your chickens"

The pastor suggested.

"What?" she said

"You keep me from giving to God?"

She it was who had pled with the bank

Upon the foreclosure following

her husband's death

Ten percent of all was granted

her of the possessions

To give to her God and her generosity she

would continue.

I learned to can chickens,

Soon many rows of jars filled shelves

in the cellar.

The best meat of chicken

In quart jars was packed.

The necks, backs plus what was left

Made jars for soup after cold packing

three hours.

Producing, preparing food with no frig.

And Everlasting Food was given.

The number gradually grew.

Sickness was rare.

One case was a miracle-

A small child recovered from cold in his lungs,

Prayers were spoken,

Prayers were answered.

Faith grew and prospered.

One day another truck moved us on

To continue the spiritual journey

After victories won.

THE FORTIETH

Since Wisconsin is next to Norway in our estimation, we had big plans for spending our fortieth wedding anniversary there. We planned to drive to Lacrosse, the area to which our ancestors immigrated centuries ago. Our compact car would make the trip just fine.

The day before our December anniversary day, we woke up to a fierce ice storm. Quickly we called the bus depot and got tickets for the trip. Then we remembered the Christmas letter from a relative in Blue Earth, Minnesota. Graciously, she offered us two large pictures in oval frames. They were portraits of our grandparents in Norway. She and her brother were adopted into the family. She decided to give them to us. We could easily stop and pick them up and that confirmed our trip to Wisconsin.

A large two-suiter suitcase was prepared containing only two blankets as we began our trip. Arriving at the Blue Earth Bus Depot, we were soon whisked away to our cousin's home for a twenty-four hour visit.

The next morning we enjoyed the awesome sight of frosted trees as we headed for La Crosse, Wisconsin. It was almost evening, dusk and chilly when we arrived. Instead of the usual bus depot in a hotel we found ourselves at the top of a very high hill. We noticed a telephone booth and a waiting booth. Both were closed. "Where will you go?" asked the driver. By the end of this trip everyone on the bus knew it was our fortieth anniversary, not too unlike the first day after our marriage. "What's a good place?" asked my husband. "Oh, the Radisson," was the reply as he pointed to it. It looked worlds away. The path would be icy and hilly. We could not call a cab with everything under lock and key for New Year's Eve. It was kind of fun standing there with that large suitcase full of antique pictures and a small suitcase containing our necessities.

Soon a very fancy limousine drove up the hill. Getting a wink from the bus driver, a man asked us "Are you wishing to go to the Radisson? I came to pick up my sister and I can swing around that way." I knew at that moment that we were of more value than a few sparrows.

The driver proved to be the goldsmith of the city. "When you get to the hotel," he said, "tell them the goldsmith sent you." Soon we found ourselves dressed in parkas and boots, in the lobby of a very fine place. The heavy suitcase came along. We wedged ourselves to the desk where a clerk laughed at us when we asked if we could get a room for the night.

As people dashed back and forth preparing for the gala events of the New Year's Eve, we sat on a bench pondering. Suddenly I said, "The man who brought us here said 'Tell them that the goldsmith sent you.'" Timidly, I approached the desk again with my plea. "By the way" I said," the goldsmith brought us here in his car." I was instructed to sit down a minute.

Soon a boy dangling a key in his hand said, "Follow me to your room." That heavenly room had a beautiful view when we opened the heavy drapes and saw the Mississippi River and the beautiful city. We soon learned we were in the Bridal Suite.

Are you aware that God takes care of His children in very special ways? Not being exactly dressed for the dinner and ballroom dance, we were not noticed as we slipped through the lobby to get out on the street.

People may have thought we were workers taking care of some details for the evening's festivities. Once outside, we looked in both directions. How wonderful-- At the end of the block we saw a Swedish Restaurant open for business.

We thanked God for the lovely meal of meatballs and Swedish pastries at exactly 7:30 PM the hour of our wedding anniversary.

HOME IN THE CITY

He had found the spouse

Following the Word received in Chicago.

His promise was "I being in the way the Lord led me."

He found the spouse long ago

Now to find the house.

The pastor's dilemma after years of

Having a parsonage provided

And with only a little money but a mustard seed faith

Plus his trust in God.

Somewhat settled in the apartment

Two sons are beginning elementary school

A wife begins her teaching responsibilities

For him, special college is ahead.

The call had come from another state

"Go forth as Abraham of old

Not knowing whither he went."

Furniture stored, the new search begins.

The opening here had come so surely, so vividly

And now God would supply needs as always.

Three weeks of searching evenings for a house so dear.

Agents shivered when they heard the story.

Finally the day came when the house was found.

Says he "There's a steel beam across

The space in the basement."

The puzzled real estate agent offered the price.

Still no money on hand for the deal

To the apartment for a hamburger meal

Family excited, bewildered and busy

This evening comes a letter in the mail

From a brother with greetings

Followed by a statement.

"Our Dad's farm is owned by six

One wants his portion

What do you wish?

I will buy your share—send you a check,"

My husband made the call from a public telephone.

Only a few days with the check in hand

He went to the agent with his wife nearby

Gave one more look at the house

With the steel beam beneath the floor

Seven years since it was built

Its condition is good.

"We'll take it" says the parson

A bewildered realtor who knows the story

Gracefully retorts: "And how will you pay?"

From the worn billfold came a check carefully folded

Almost half the price of the house

With big eyes and neck turning red

The man assents, staring into space

"God gave us a house we did not build"

Was the only explanation offered.

Next day after school, the business was done

The down payment showed lack of experience

The realtor suggested holding back some,

Unexpected expenses may be ahead.

Settled in the first home we ever owned

Was a happy family of four

Living there for eighteen years was a pleasure

Sons grown, attended college and achieved

Parents growing older, looking to the future.

Again, seeing an agent

We found our dream home in the city

Larger rooms, conventional dining room

Two fireplaces, plenty of yard

Once again the way has opened

Once again the miracle was seen

The price is cut, the old home is sold

The three years of rental

Only increased its value

Now to the mortgage company he went.

The money in his pocket

A grin on his face

All debts he will today erase.

The God who would not fail

Would be faithful to the end.

He had prepared blessings untold

For one who trusted in Him.

IT'S GOLDEN

How does a couple remain happily married for fifty years? Loving, not only in word but in deed. Marriage began in Genesis and has not yet ended. The right relationship results in great happiness. One must be committed to the needs of the other and to love regardless of circumstances. The third Person, the Holy Spirit, comforts through sickness and health, through poverty and riches. Ecclesiastes says, "A threefold cord is not quickly broken." We realized how blest we were and we made the decision! It was our golden wedding and we would travel to Norway to celebrate.

Several times we had visited Norway and a lovely cousin visited us in the summertime. She invited us to see Norway for Yuletide. We left Sioux Falls on December 29 1992, flying KLM over Newfoundland, across the Atlantic to Scotland, and then over the North Sea to make the connection for Oslo, Norway. Once in Oslo, Ole took us in his Renault over the countryside to Brandval. Christmas candles and outdoor- lighted trees lit the dark Norwegian sky. By mid-afternoon USA time, but early

Norwegian time, we were bedded down under down tick comforters.

Soon after the long rest, we enjoyed sights, smells, sounds and tastes of Norway besides the wonderful fellowship with many slekten. We were in "Finnskogen" the area where grandmother Olivia emigrated from to Bridgewater, South Dakota. The beautiful forest and mountains spoke loudly to me as Ole showed us the shops, relatives and the area. Fifty years ago, we would not have believed we would be in Europe for our golden Anniversary.

On the day of December 31, we had coffee with many relatives after which Olaug prepared a lovely meal of salmon, boiled potatoes, vegetables and a dessert of prune pudding. The treat came later when we enjoyed an ice cream cake in the shape of a horseshoe for good luck on our matrimonial day.

This anniversary, too, we attended church. I felt I had been in church so many New Year's eves that this time we would just relax and celebrate. The hound of heaven was on my path as Olaug said: "Would it be all right if we attend Brandval Kirk before we have our meal?" Sure. After the service, all in Norwegian, I was honored to place a lighted candle on the grave of an ancestor. We were warned that there would be fire works at midnight. Somehow, I felt that it was a celebration at the end of our special day.

The next day in Kongsberg, I was invited to have a honeymoon ride. The hill was very icy and I was sitting on a Spork. Leonard pushed or held back the sled. What fun!

In touring, we witnessed so many highlights including a train trip to Drammen where we saw the church built in the 1600s by Daniel Knoff. We sang and played the piano in Homes for the Elderly. Leonard spoke at a chapel service in the Fjellen Haug Mission School. It was our pleasure to meet missionaries who are trained here, to serve around the world. A few days in the Pensjonat and after the two weeks, we returned to our own Home Sweet Home.

TOGETHER

The nursing home attendant handed us the bibs. The bright blue binding around them looked quite nice. My sister Lillian's bib was exactly the same as mine. There was only a two-year difference in our ages and many thought we were twins. I was aware that our voices, as well as our profile with the small round nose and the almost identical sound of our voices, gave us likeness.

I had come four hundred miles to pay this visit of tribute to my eighty-eight year old sister. She is the last of my siblings. We were from a family of nine children and now we two remained like fragile leaves clinging to a good branch.

I spent the better part of the day with Lillian in the Senior Care Center. She brightened only briefly when I appeared at 9:30 am. The response to my greeting was muffled and not understandable. Speak of helplessness… I felt it deeply. I pulled a chair up beside her wheel chair, placed my warm hand on her cold arm and she looked pleased. For some minutes, we just sat there looking at each other and waiting.

Then through an outburst of tears Lillian said, "Don't know why I am here. Don't know what I am doing." Spells of crying followed. Soon the tears were flowing from both her eyes and mine. "The crying is inside of me," she said. The crying had begun to come from inside of me also.

There are no good answers to the questions she may have, but I sat calmly, often holding her hand or patting her shoulder. "We are both older now," I said, "It's good we have good care. This is a place of care giving." I assured her that the attendants here love her and are making it better for her. My comment or its equal was repeated during the morning. By noon, she unexpectedly said to two nurses "Thank you for the wonderful care you have given me."

It seemed longer than a few hours. Finally, I asked a nurse if there was a piano nearby. She directed me to a lovely Kawai keyboard in the lounge. I played the piano for her when she resided in the city where I lived until about six months ago. Now with a roomful of residents listening, clapping and calling for more, she seemed to be fastening her eyes on me at the piano. At the first sound, she had a tear in her eye and a very slight smile on her face, "You're welcome as the flowers on Blueberry Hill" seemed to be a hit so I played it in several variations. Then I went into patriotic numbers as "America", "Battle Hymn of the Republic" and more. Well-known hymns included "What a Friend" "Children of the Heavenly Father" and "The Love of God." Then there was a request from the large man with the striped suspenders. "Do 'Blueberry Hill' again." I played it gladly. The piano concert may have been more for my benefit than for that of any one else. Lillian may have soaked in some of the numbers. Then there was clapping and thanks from the attending nurse.

Soon I was rolling my sister's wheel chair back to Wing Three. This was the area for residents with Alzheimer's problems and it was a lock in area. I used the code to enter it. We were seated in the dining area and soon a white Turkish bib with blue binding was fastened around our necks. There were only a few residents here. They have been wheeled in to eat around four tables. My sister's food has been ground and mashed. I had asked to have the same serving as she had but my tray contained the regular menu. During this mealtime there were disturbing noises and a loud "Hurry up" from someone. A chilling scream startled me. Nevertheless, I picked at my meat loaf and the sliced potatoes. I missed the seasoning and no saltshaker was evident. The red, diced beets were quite appealing. Her food had not been touched. Finally, an attendant persuaded her to take a few small mouthfuls. Her own spoonfuls, which she attempted to handle, were about one sixth of a small teaspoonful. I managed to give her some liquid supplement that she sucked up through a straw. This was the most successful. As I kept chewing a little, I fought guilty feelings for the good food and the wonderful environment I enjoyed at the Retirement Community where I lived. During the mealtime there were disturbing noises and a loud "hurry up" from someone.

I must accept the fact of her disease: the slight tremor from Parkinson's, her loss of hearing and the memory loss caused by the Alzheimer's sickness. My prayer is for her comfort. My concern is for her weight loss, which is a big factor in her survival.

Back in her small but beautiful room, I sat in a straight chair beside her. She seemed to doze off several times. Once she called out loudly, "Who wants something?" "What can I do?" As I sat there admiring the lovely pictures on her walls, the decorations so carefully furnished, I wondered, "What can I do?" "Dear Lord, what would you have me do?" I do not understand but I will continue to hope and to pray to the One so much wiser than I.

An hour later, the bus driver came to take me back to the motel where I was staying these few days. I left reluctantly, feeling great helplessness but also having the satisfaction that I had tried to ease the suffering a little. I have become more aware and more understanding.

I left the collection of reminiscent magazine pictures I collected for her. They were fastened to tag board, all in loose form to be easily handled. They were applied with non-toxic stickers from the scrapbook store. They included a few things true to our home background. There was the old Monarch range on which Mother cooked the good meals, the back yard swing set, fashions, food and more. Lillian ignored them. Per chance she may look at one some day, it will be worthwhile.

The greatest longing is for home and I assured her that one day we will join our family in that Heavenly Home. The good-bye is brief   --a kiss and a hug and "I'll see you in the morning."

Ten days later my niece called me... "I'm visiting my mother" she said. "She is talking about the pictures you brought to her."

DOILY JOURNAL

My interest in Hardanger stitchery relates to beginnings. Early childhood is fascinating with the eagerness and the joy of accomplishment. Even in my early years I was curious about stitchery. Mother encouraged that by furnishing simple supplies to begin a very small project. Nothing pleases a mother or a teacher more than to see the "I did it myself" expression on the face of a child! Likewise, the klosters made with satin stitches begin the Hardanger design. Carefully and accurately one makes the grill on which the embroidery will be done. The design has been begun. Following the klosters there must be a plan for the cutting process. There will be no mistakes in the cutting process. Incorrect stitches can be removed and redone with great effort. Children and the beginnings of life must also be done with great and tender loving care. The weaving and the wrapping of the doily being made requires patience. Our children, who are of the greatest value that we will ever have, remain until they like us pass the doily on to another generation.

GOD'S HOME

My son's small hands were tightened around my neck as I held him in my arms. We were moving along in the darkness on a boardwalk from the church to our home. The end of a wearisome Sunday it was. Three services were held on this day, concluding with the late evening one. I, along with my pastor husband, had poured out my heart. Did anyone care? I was Sunday school teacher, pianist, children's worker and hostess for two tables filled with guests at noon.

"Why are we doing this when such little results are being realized?" I asked myself . Then it was that the chubby hands clutched my neck and turned my face upwards toward the evening sky.

"God's at home tonight," he said.

"Why did you say that?" I asked.

"See!" he said, "The lights are on!" And he pointed to the night sky twinkling with millions of stars.

The God of the sky said, "Be not weary." God is in control and all is right with the world. I'm so glad. GOD'S HOME!

PRECIOUS MOMENTS

One cold day in January, my granddaughter and I were lying on the bed relaxing. There had been several weeks of togetherness so conversation went rather deep. Old times were discussed along with important concepts of family. She wanted to know who married who and stories of the old days.

"Grandma," she said, "when you got married did your name change?" 'Yes, dear," I responded. "You see my name was Evelyn Dirks and when I married Grandpa Leonard, I became Evelyn Knoff or Mrs. Leonard Knoff." "Is this the way everyone does it when they get married?" she said after a quiet moment. Her big, four-year-old eyes were searching mine.

"Oh my," she said, "That will be a problem for me."

"Oh no," I responded, "When that time in your life comes, it will be just the way it will be. It won't be any problem."

"You don't understand. It will be a problem for me!" she exclaimed.

"You see, I don't know Mark's last name."

Send a Doll

It was only three days after the funeral. A dear little friend aged seven had been hit by a car and died. So it was that the little five-year-old girl came to Grandma's house. "I have to see you," she said. Safely in Grandma's bedroom with the door tightly closed, she quickly drew a small six-inch doll from under her shirt. "Here, Grandma," she said, "Give this to my friend when you get to heaven."

The precious child continued: "You know, grandma, you are older than I am and you will probably get there first. Just give it to him!"

As her Grandma my first thoughts were that we don't take anything with us. But looking into her tender, longing eyes, I simply said, "Yes, dear. I'll put it right here on the closet shelf to take it with me." She added: "Great Grandma is holding him on her lap now and reading stories to him".

What a big faith for a little girl! Faith in Heaven, in the assurance that her friend is there, that I will be there and she will follow, besides the knowledge that Great Grandma is safely with Jesus.

VELMA'S CAT

As a young child, I yearned to take piano lessons from the doctor's wife in our town. No way! Only an old pump organ with one pedal working and I was so short I had to stand to reach it. Still I was picking out a few tunes.

There really wasn't twenty-five cents a week to be spent on something like piano lessons. With eight children to feed and clothe, each penny in our home was spent wisely. My Dad was a grain elevator manager, but crops were failing and so was his income.

With four cows in a pasture on the edge of our village, my mother eked out extra money by selling milk to almost everyone in town. I did have a share in earning the family income. I delivered one quart of milk to each household daily and received eight cents for each delivery. Being a milk man or milk gal when my legs were so short had its problems. "Mom," I said, "the snow banks are too deep. I can't get my legs up for the next step." Mom accepted no excuses. "Get the milk to each house before school," was her order.

One glorious day my mother was visiting with Velma, the doctor's wife. An arrangement was made that day that changed my whole life.

You see, Velma had a beautiful white Persian cat. The cat needed milk daily. Also, Velma was the music teacher in our town. It was decided that I would bring one pint of milk to the doctor's door each morning for six days of the week for the cat. On Sunday, they would get along. That milk was worth four cents per delivery. The piano lessons were priced at twenty-five cents each. This generous piano teacher called it even! She supplied lots of music books and gave me very special attention while her white Persian cat purred nearby.

Doc and Velma became very special mentors for me. I continued the piano lessons for years. When I graduated from the eighth grade, I was proud of the lovely blue cotton dress with a peplum around the waist that Velma made for me..

I continued my interest in music my entire life. Extra lessons in college and becoming a pianist in many churches that my husband and I served gave me good experience. My husband was a soloist and I accompanied him for small and large occasions. It was a joy for me to lead in the Christmas programs in public schools and church services. My entire life was enriched with good experiences as a pianist.

Velma and Doc made a lasting impression and contribution to my joy of living. Only after many years did I have the privilege of locating Velma and thanking her for her blessing on my life.

THE SHOES HAVE IT

I was the queen of the first grade room in Eugene Field School. It was the fall of 1954 and it was my first year of teaching school in the city. My heart leapt with joy, but after two days with thirty-six six-year-olds, I was overwhelmed with the responsibility of completing the curriculum daily and keeping the children occupied and happy.

I went to the Principal's office and said: "Can you please hire a substitute teacher for a few days at my expense? I need to do some observing and learning."

"Oh no," he said. "You are IT and you are doing just fine." Little did he know that my whole lifetime of experience had already been exhausted!

That evening while my young sons bought their school supplies, I scouted around at a shoe store. "That's it," I said, as I spotted the size seven, shiny red high-heeled shoes. "That's it! Shoes for a Queen" I said and I purchased them.

I can picture the classroom even today: six tables each containing six compartments for supplies, and myself confidently teaching in the red shoes. The challenge was ever before me. Not only were the children learning, I was growing and learning too.

One of my loves, as well as the children's, was music. Blessed with a piano in my classroom, I often stepped over to it and led such famous songs as "If you're happy and you know it, clap your hands" and "From the Halls of Montezuma to the Shores of Tripoli, we will fight our country's battles on the land and on the sea." We sang with gusto! And this teacher wore her shiny, red high-heeled shoes daily.

Reading, writing and arithmetic were not ignored in the midst of all this fun. One impressed mother came to me with tears running down her cheeks, "My child is reading!" she cried. It had not occurred to me that some first graders might not learn to read.

The love of art was also high in the children's curriculum. I tried to touch all the bases. Occasionally, I mixed watercolors. How magic could things be when red and yellow turned to orange, red and blue produced purple, and blue and yellow became green? As the time for cleanup came, my feet were killing me and my head ached. But what an honor it was for the child chosen to be on the cleanup committee. They all looked pleased with their accomplishment. And this teacher in the red, high-heeled shoes was exhausted.

Aware of the children's responses and lack of them, I noticed Joey who was on the clean up committee. He had never spoken to me, never uttered a single word. Following the clean up, I helped him button his jacket and put on his warm mittens. Suddenly he blurted out, "My mom has a job now!" Could this home problem have caused his extreme quietness? Or was it his fear of leaving home for this new world of education? But now he was speaking!

Encouraged, I said, "Good, where does she work?" I was delighted that he was talking. The tired feet in the shiny, red high-heeled shoes did not hurt so much now.

After telling me where his mother worked, he smilingly left my classroom, but not until he had turned his head my way and said, "Mrs. Knoff, where do YOU work?"

DOILY JOURNAL

"Precious in the sight of the Lord is the death of His saints."
Psalm 116:15

Facing death with loved ones has given me a glance, not only of the tunnel we will all enter but of the glories that await God's children. Likewise, the stitchery has been completed. The errors have been redeemed. The edging is complete. The cutting away process is the separation of the doily from its background. No longer the need for the support given to each detail. The cutting away from this world is the separation of life from the earthly to the heavenly. Life emerges as does a butterfly from its cocoon. No need for the material things but only the freedom that has come with the flight to heaven. My real self will be ready to glorify my Father in Heaven. "Well done" will be the final word. The separation of one's self will mean everlasting freedom.

CRITICAL SUPPORT

Did I make the correct response to the question my brother-in-law asked me: "Should I consent to remove the support system from your sister Esther?"

Esther, the loving, giving and efficient nurse, missionary to Nigeria, the gifted pianist who surrendered her playing because her arthritic hands no longer allowed it. My beloved sister. And now found unconscious, rushed to a Denver hospital and placed on life support on that April morning in 2005.

Then days were spent grieving and calling to find out that her condition was unchanged. Periodically specialists in the critical care unit reported that extensive brain damage had occurred due to periods of insufficient oxygen.

Seven hundred miles separated us and I could do little but pray.

After fourteen days in this comatose condition, the doctors agreed that she probably would not regain consciousness and that unless we want to care for her in this condition (indefinitely) we should remove all life supports. The final decision was made by Charles, her husband.

My response was always "Charles, whatever you decide I will support you." What a difficult decision.

We talked more and more, and then God gave me the answer. "Charles. What do you think Esther would decide?"

Quickly, he responded, "She would want no tubes to keep her alive." My response was: "That may be the answer."

The hospital personnel asked me to speak to my sister before the supports were removed, and the arrangements were made. They advised, however, that she probably would not be aware of the conversation.

I could not give Esther that final message until I asked my pastor to pray for my strength and for wisdom.

I took a deep breath and picked up the phone. "Esther," I simply said, "This is Evelyn. I love you very much. You are going HOME. It will be wonderful. You will breathe ethereal air. There will be no pain or grief. I commit you to Him who does all things well. You will be with our parents and family who have gone on before. Please greet them and tell them we will be coming to join them. You will be forever in our Savior's care. The Lord will reach out His hand to you and, as you reach your hand to Him, it will be perfectly whole. I love you. Goodbye."

The hardest part was that there was no response. I waited…and waited…and waited.

It was the most silent moment I have ever heard.

AFTERGLOW

The message seemed to be coming out loud and clear. Only ten percent of his heart was functioning and my 86-year-old husband's death was imminent. Months? Weeks? "No," says our doctor, "days and maybe only a few. Make your preparations. Call your family."

God loves him even more than I do and I began to relinquish my hold on him. His surrender is complete and mine must be likewise. Fighting for breath, he expresses that at times it feels like a sack has been placed over his head. What a sacrifice of praise as he continued to pray and care for his family, his church and for the congregations of the past!

I returned home from the hospital at 9:30 pm, I saw the "lived in" scene on our kitchen table. Various non-edible things were there. The red glass container may not be needed for his medicine water any more. I washed it and put it away. The antique saltcellar that held his eight to ten pills is no longer necessary. The magnifying glass used to read devotions and the Argus Leader went back to the study. The cup with horses on it that he received for a recent birthday will remain.

The second day of his hospitalization Leonard reported to his doctor that he saw stars in his eyes. Those beautiful hazel eyes! I had a feeling that the lights were going out.

God was very near to both of us at this time. We felt an unusual strength as together we faced death. Strong support from our sons and other family members brought peace and a glorious expression to his face. Pastors, who visited Leonard faithfully with their songs and prayers, helped with the overcoming. One moment he told me that he was "Glory Bound." Remembering prayer and comfort he had brought to many gave us peace.

All evening he moved endlessly, pulling sheets and blankets until he was fenced in. He seemed to understand as I held his bony head in my two hands. Once I said "We're holding hands." "Kleenex" he said. As I handed the tissue to him I said: "Blow your nose? Or spit?" He very gently and in a moment of alertness, took the tissue to the edge of his right eye, with a slight wink, and he wiped a tear away. We understood our mutual feelings of love.

At one moment of desperation, I again cradled his head in my hands and said "Leonard, God is our Refuge and Strength in times of trouble and we are in trouble." Then I had the last prayer with my husband.

The long and difficult night passed. Dawn had broken. All movement had ceased. I wanted to place a kiss on his forehead or at least to pat his hand, but I felt I should not disturb the peaceful rest. The ultimate healing had come. There was no more pain. There was no struggle and no deep breath. His soul had made its flight to God.

Only peace pervaded the scene. I finally placed a kiss on his forehead and then dropped to my knees at his bedside. In a very feeble and thin voice I sang one verse of our favorite song "I'd Rather Have Jesus Than Anything." Our pastor joined my son and myself as we prayed and rejoiced in the midst of our sorrow. During the course of the hour, David prayed saying, "Please tell Dad we miss him but we are glad he is with You and You are with us." We are experiencing the afterglow of a life lived for Christ.

My home did not seem empty as I entered it. I knew there was a separation as I braced myself to be an anchor for my family. "What a household of God" Leonard would have said as a circle of friendship began to surround me.

Could I just curl up somewhere and cry? The day pushed me forward with the writing of the obituary, the calls I made for casket bearers and musicians. It all faced me with force but I was given grace and strength to go through it step by step. I looked for a sheet of paper to make a list of things to be done. In his lined table was the unfinished letter to a grand daughter in Stanford University. "January twenty-ninth, I read your letter. It sounds like you have a heavy schedule you are taking, especially calculus and chemistry. The resources of God are great." There was no completion, no signing "Grandpa" but it showed real love from an elderly gentleman to his granddaughter.

The afterglow of his life showed on a beautiful countenance as we viewed his body in the funeral parlor. The mortician said he did not want to change the countenance on his face. We rejoiced at the peaceful serenity and victory.

Now we planned the funeral service. Music was very important in our lives. Our organist consented to put special emphasis on "A Mighty Fortress is our God " during the entrance hymn. Our sister-in-law from Grand Forks will sing: "Behold the Host" in both English and Norwegian and she will also sing "The Lord's Prayer." Also, we planned for Leonard via tape to sing "It is Well with My Soul." He made a special tape of this hymn on his eighty-fifth birthday.

I felt strengthened as I remembered how we started to sing "I'd Rather have Jesus." It was July tenth of 1942. I was preparing to go to church on a Sunday morning. There was a knock on my door. Standing in the doorway was a church lady who said, "This young man will sing at the morning service. Could you accompany him on the piano?" I heard myself say, "Yes, I guess I could." I would never have dreamed that I would be accompanying him at the piano and throughout life for 56 years.

God's Presence was very real during the funeral week. The service was strengthening although I find it impossible to explain what it feels like to sit on the front pew for a funeral service. As the tape of Leonard's was singing, the text soaked into my heart..."Though Satan should buffet...Lord, hasten the day when the clouds shall be rolled away." I felt frailty and victory all in one.

At the graveside service I placed a flower and a kiss on the casket saying, "I send my love with you Leonard." As we left the scene that day a casket bearer whispered in my ear "Rejoice".

There was a tremendous sense of loss as I realized the recent happenings. My body grew weary and weak. Remembrances kept coming through me with every step that I took. I found much comfort from those, both young and old, who told me and wrote telling me of their acceptance of Christ through his life and ministry. There was therapy for me in writing letters and thank you notes and writing in my journal.

I BELIEVE

It was a late Monday afternoon exactly three weeks after my husband's funeral. I was finding myself weary and relaxed in my recliner. It ended with my leaning way back, watching a "nothing" program on TV and waiting for the news. I was soon in a deep sleep with an afghan comfortably covering me.

Suddenly, I felt startled and quickly sat up straight in my chair. I saw a figure—flimsy, silky and transparent. It was developing as I watched. It was about three feet in height and about six feet from me. As I gazed, I felt filled with a bright light. Soon I recognized my husband's pleasant face. The hazel eyes twinkled at me. Even as I stared, the old salmon-colored jacket that was familiar to me framed the figure. The face and the figure I would have known anywhere. He loved to wear that jacket in-doors as well as out-of-doors. The knowing smile made me feel warm and thrilled. Then suddenly I witnessed a little light dance and I saw him no more. I was filled with peace and wonder.

I will go to the garage where the jacket has been placed in a box for the Salvation Army. It will now remain in the back of my closet. The joy of the countenance will remain in my heart.

I BELIEVE IN MY ANGEL!

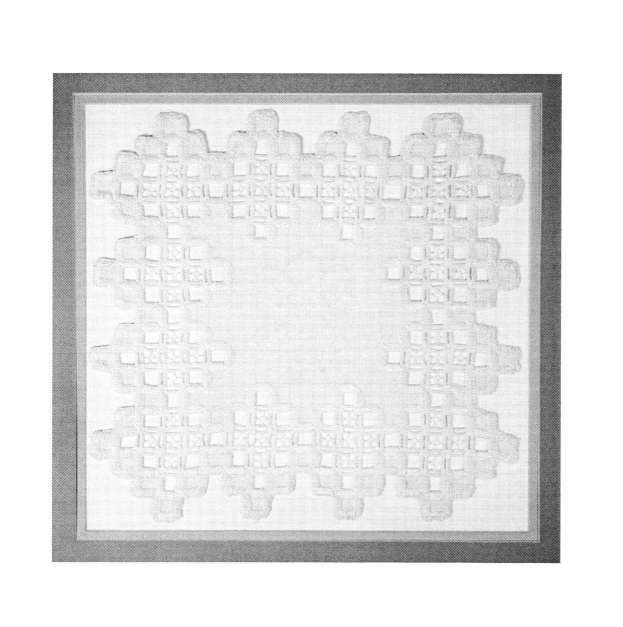